John Rutter

Lo, how a Rose e'er blooming

(Es ist ein' Ros' entsprungen)

Oboe and piano

OXFORD

Lo, how a Rose e'er blooming

(Es ist ein' Ros' entsprungen)

JOHN RUTTER
based on a German chorale melody

Lo, how a Rose e'er blooming
(Es ist ein' Ros' entsprungen)

JOHN RUTTER
based on a German chorale melody

OXFORD UNIVERSITY PRESS MUSIC DEPARTMENT, GREAT CLARENDON STREET, OXFORD OX2 6DP